Managing Editor
Karen Goldfluss, M.S. Ed.

Editor-in-Chief
Sharon Coan, M.S. Ed.

Illustrator
Renée Christine Yates

Cover Artist
Barb Lorseyedi

Art Manager
Kevin Barnes

Art Director
CJae Froshay

Imaging
James Edward Grace
Rosa C. See
Richard Easily

Product Manager
Phil Garcia

Publisher
Mary D. Smith, M.S. Ed.

Full

Literacy Activities

Math

Teacher Created Resources

Author

Lorin Klistoff, M.A.

Teacher Created Resources, Inc.
6421 Industry Way
Westminster, CA 92683
www.teachercreated.com.
ISBN-0-7439-3170-X
©2004 Teacher Created Resources, Inc.
Reprinted, 2006
Made in U.S.A.

Table of Contents

Introduction

Literacy Activities: Math is a wonderful addition to any first or second grade math curriculum. This book was created especially for the busy teachers of young students. The hands-on, developmentally appropriate activities are sure to provide your students with fun-filled learning experiences. The activities are full color and will add some spice to the regular classroom material. The contents in the book provide a variety of ways to reinforce math concepts and skills while maintaining student interest. The activities are easy to implement with little or no preparation at all. The activities are meant to support and be a resource for teachers as they teach these content skills. The activities provide review and practice in the following areas of math:

- identifying shapes and their characteristics
- creating simple patterns
- identifying numbers 1–100 or from 100–999
- identifying place value
- counting by 10s, 5s, and 2s
- greater than, less than, and equal to
- using ordinal numbers
- time on the hour, on the half-hour, and to the minute
- add, subtract, and multiply whole numbers
- understanding commonly used fractions
- solving real-world word problems
- counting money
- reading and interpreting simple charts and graphs
- measuring in inches or to the nearest centimeter

Each activity is set up with an easy-to-follow lesson. First, each lesson states the objective or learning skill and the materials needed. Most of the materials are provided inside this book. Next, the lesson outlines in what kinds of groupings the activity can be implemented. Most of the activities can be adapted in multiple ways and can be "custom tailored." They can be implemented as a whole-class lesson, as a small-group lesson, in partners, independently, or in a math center. The activities can also be adapted for a variety of student levels. Suggestions are listed in the actual directions of the activity or they are suggested in the "Ideas" section. The "Ideas" section contains many helpful hints on such things as storage of materials or ideas to either enhance or extend the activity.

The activities are based on the latest math standards. Just cut out the pieces needed to create great-looking learning centers or fun-filled games. Laminate them for years of use. Follow the step-by-step directions, and watch the learning take place!

Shape Riddler

 ## Skill

* understanding basic properties of simple geometric shapes

 ## Student Grouping

* partner
* center
* small group
* whole group

Materials

* one set of Riddle Cards (page 5 and/or page 9)
* one set of Shape Cards (page 7 and/or page 11)

Directions

1. Lay the shape cards face up on a flat surface. (*Note:* If you are working with a large group, you may want to enlarge the Shape Cards and tape them to the board for all students to see. Or, you may want to draw the shapes directly on a chalkboard or whiteboard.)

2. Mix up the Riddle Cards.

3. Place the Riddle Cards in a pile face down.

4. A student (or teacher) chooses a Riddle Card.

5. A student (or teacher) reads the Riddle Card and then picks somebody to guess the shape. If the person guesses incorrectly, give another student a chance to guess. Continue guessing until the correct shape is chosen. (*Note:* The answers are located at the bottom of each Riddle Card.)

6. The next player (or teacher) chooses another Riddle Card.

7. Repeat the process until all the Riddle Cards are finished.

 ## Ideas

* Laminate the Riddle and Shape Cards for durability.
* Copy the Riddle and Shape Cards to create more sets.
* Use only pages 5 and 7 for children who are just beginning to understand the properties of basic shapes.
* Have students play Shapes Ahoy! on page 13 after completing this activity.

Riddle Cards

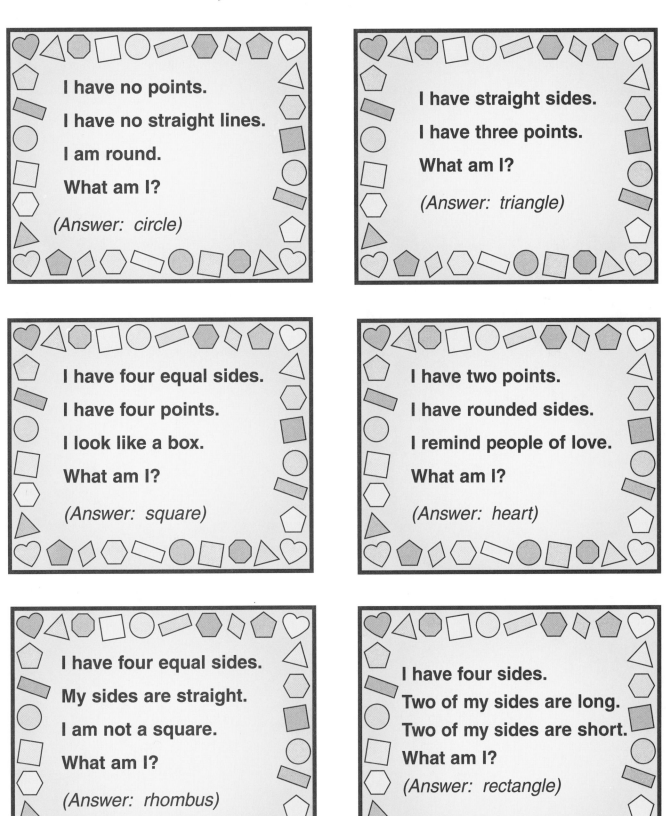

I have no points.

I have no straight lines.

I am round.

What am I?

(Answer: circle)

I have straight sides.

I have three points.

What am I?

(Answer: triangle)

I have four equal sides.

I have four points.

I look like a box.

What am I?

(Answer: square)

I have two points.

I have rounded sides.

I remind people of love.

What am I?

(Answer: heart)

I have four equal sides.

My sides are straight.

I am not a square.

What am I?

(Answer: rhombus)

I have four sides.

Two of my sides are long.

Two of my sides are short.

What am I?

(Answer: rectangle)

Shape Cards

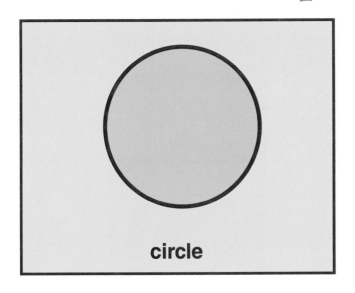

circle

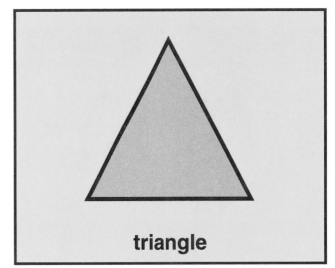

triangle

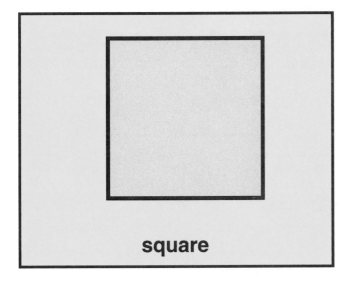

square

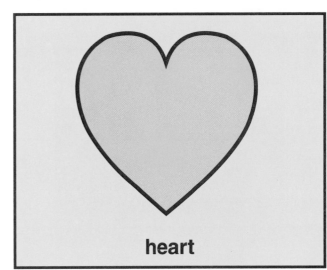

heart

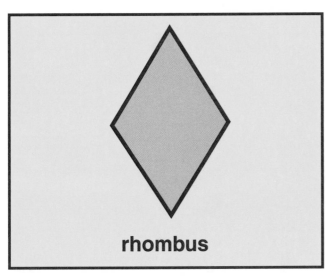

rhombus

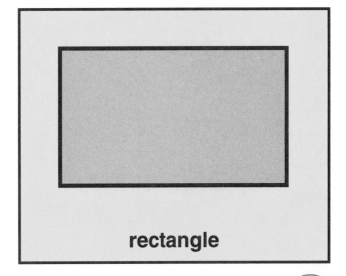

rectangle

Riddle Cards

I have five points.

I have five corners.

My sides are equal.

What am I?

(Answer: pentagon)

I have six points.

I have six corners.

My sides are equal.

What am I?

(Answer: hexagon)

I have eight points.

I have eight corners.

My sides are equal.

What am I?

(Answer: octagon)

I have a circle for my bottom.

I have a circle for my top.

I sometimes hold soup inside me.

What am I?

(Answer: cylinder)

I have no points.

My shape is a ball.

What am I?

(Answer: sphere)

I have a circle for my bottom.

A point is at the top.

People can put ice cream on me.

What am I?

(Answer: cone)

#3170 Math Literacy Activities

Shape Cards

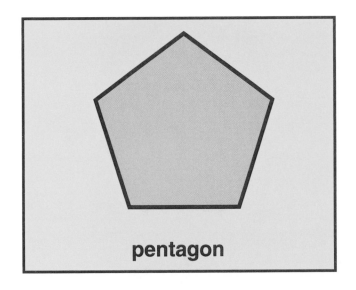

pentagon

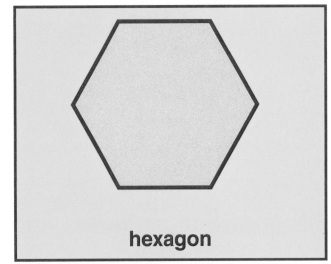

hexagon

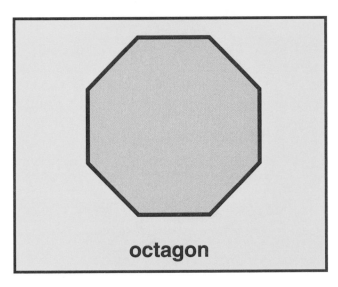

octagon

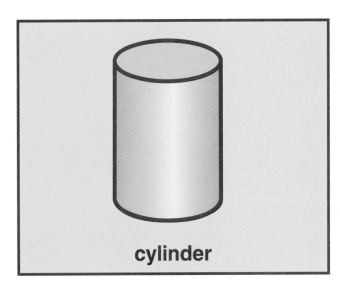

cylinder

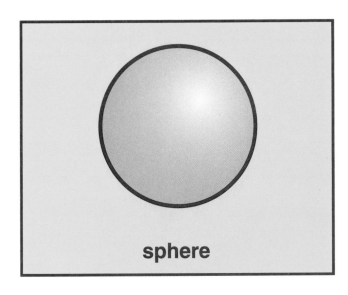

sphere

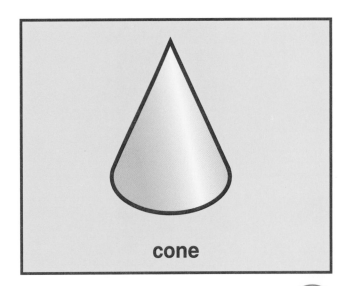

cone

Skill

* identifying two- and three-dimensional geometric shapes

Student Grouping

* partners

* center

* small group

Materials

* 1 copy of Shapes Ahoy! Game Board (page 15)

* playing marker for each player

* die with only the numbers 1, 2, and 3

Directions

1. The first player rolls the die and moves that number forward.

2. He or she must read the name of the shape on which the marker landed. Then he or she must name an object that has that shape. For instance, if he or she landed on the octagon, he or she must say "octagon—stop sign." Allow the student to ask other students for ideas if he or she gets stumped.

3. The next player rolls the die and moves that number forward and repeats the same process.

4. The game continues until one player (or all players) reaches "Finish."

Ideas

* Laminate the game board for durability, especially when using in a math center.

* Prior to this activity, play Shape Riddler on page 4.

* Prior to starting the game, have students bring in objects from home which contain the shapes included on the board (Example: can of soup = cylinder). Discuss all the attributes of the object. This will help them feel more confident when playing the game.

* Make multiple copies of the game board and have more dice available if using with the whole class.

* Have each student create his or her own shapes game board.

Shapes Ahoy! Game Board

Directions: Roll the die. Move your marker the correct number of spaces. Say the name of the shape on which you landed. The first one to reach "Finish" is the winner.

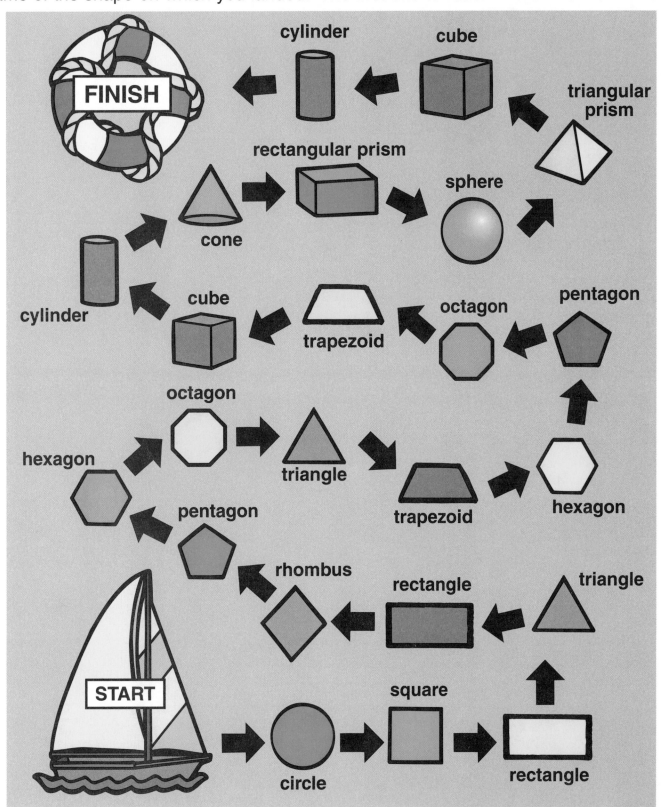

Crack the Code

 Skill

✳ understanding and creating simple patterns

 Student Grouping

✳ partners

✳ small group

✳ center

 Materials

✳ Pattern Code Cards (page 19)

✳ Shape Cards (page 21), Object Cards (page 23), and/or two copies of Number Cards (page 47)

 Directions

1. Mix the Pattern Code Cards and place face down on a flat surface.

2. The first player picks a Pattern Code Card.

3. The first player must create a pattern from Numbers, Shapes, and/or Object Cards according to the pattern code stated on the Pattern Code Card.

4. When the first player finishes his or her pattern, the other players must check it to see if it is correct.

5. Then the second player picks a Pattern Code Card and repeats the process.

6. After the game is finished and all Pattern Code Cards are used, have each student create his or her own pattern from the Number, Shape, and/or Object Cards and have the other players guess the code.

 Ideas

✳ Laminate all cards for durability, especially if using in a center.

✳ Copy a set of the pattern code cards and number/shape/object cards for each student to use for a whole-class lesson.

✳ Try using other manipulatives to make patterns such as pattern blocks, markers, or beads. Have students record their pattern code underneath their patterns.

✳ Have students create patterns and have a partner continue the pattern.

ABBABB

AABAAB

AABCAABC

ABCCABCC

ABAB

ABCABC

ABBCABBC

AABBAABB

#3170 Math Literacy Activities

#3170 Math Literacy Activities

Shape Cards

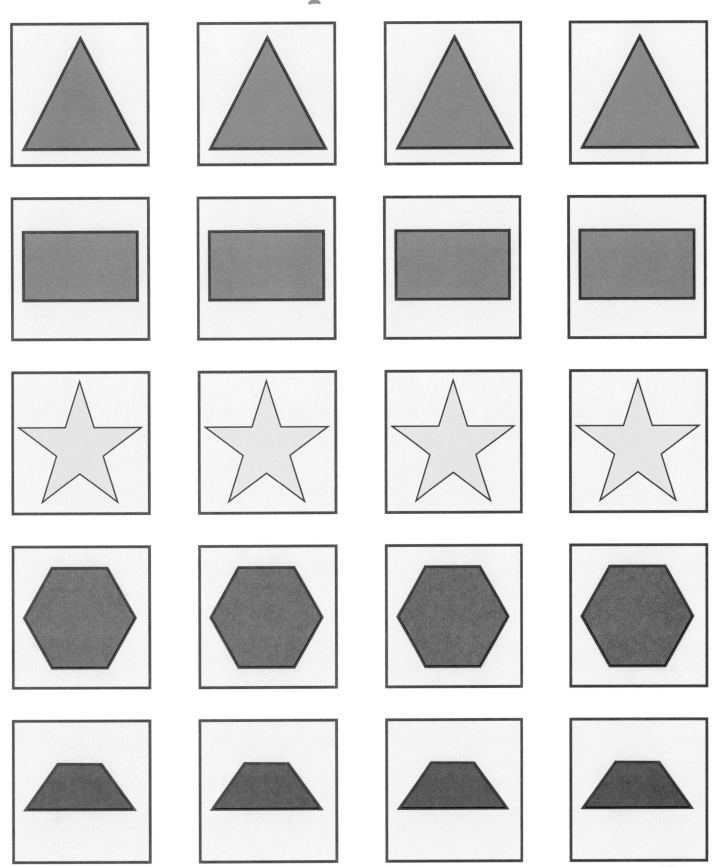

Object Cards

 # Memory Match

 ## Skill

* understanding that numbers are symbols used to represent quantities
* reading number names 0–25

 ## Student Grouping

* independent
* small group
* partners
* center

Materials

* appropriate number cards from pages 27–35

 ## Directions

1. Choose one of the following ways to play this game depending on your students' needs:

   * match number to object
   * match words to objects
   * match number to word
   * match words, numbers, and objects

2. Mix up and lay all cards face down on a flat surface.

3. The first player picks two (or three depending on game played) cards. If the cards match (Example: two and 2), the player keeps the match. If there is no match made, the first player flips the cards face down. Other players should try and remember what was shown on those cards.

4. Next, the second player picks two (or three depending on game played) cards. If the cards match, the player keeps the match. If there is no match made, the second player flips the cards face down. Other players should try to remember the locations of cards.

5. The game continues until all matches are found.

6. The player with the most matches is the winner.

Ideas

* Laminate cards and store in small, plastic bag for durability.

* Encourage students to count by 2s, 3s, or 5s when counting objects on the cards.

* Place all number word cards in a pile. Pick a number word card and have students write a sentence using the number word chosen. For example, if the number "three" is picked, a student might write "I have three brothers." Have them illustrate each sentence and make their own number books. If students are more advanced, pick two number word cards and have them create word problems. For example, if the number cards "five" and "seven" were chosen, a student might write "Jason had five apples. Jane had seven apples. How many apples were there altogether?"

* Copy a set of cards for all students and use for other math lessons. For example, use the number and object cards to help support an addition lesson.

1	one	
2	two	
3	three	
4	four	
5	five	

6	**six**	
7	**seven**	
8	**eight**	
9	**nine**	
10	**ten**	

11	**eleven**	
12	**twelve**	
13	**thirteen**	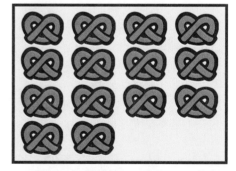
14	**fourteen**	
15	**fifteen**	

16	sixteen	
17	seventeen	
18	eighteen	
19	nineteen	
20	twenty	

21	twenty-one	
22	twenty-two	
23	twenty-three	
24	twenty-four	
25	twenty-five	

Outer Space Walk

 ## Skill

* identifying numbers (1–100 or 100–999)

Student Grouping

* partners
* small group
* center

 ## Materials

* Outer Space Walk game board (pages 40 and 41)
* playing marker for each player
* die with the numbers 1, 2, and 3

Directions

1. Tape pages 40 and 41 together to create the complete game board.

2. Write the number 1–100 in the craters. If you would like to make it challenging, write various numbers from 100–999 in the craters.

3. Place all markers at the "START."

4. The first player rolls the die and moves the designated number of spaces.

5. The first player must say the name of the number on which he or she landed.

6. Then the second player rolls the die and moves the designated number of spaces.

7. The second player must say the name of the number on which he or she landed.

8. Continue playing until one player (or all players) has reached "FINISH."

 ## Ideas

* Laminate the game board for durability, especially if using in a center.

* Other game options include the following: (1) Each player must say how many tens and/or how many ones are in each number on which his or her marker landed. (2) Each player must say two factors of the number on which his or her marker landed. For example, the number 32 could be 8 and 4. (3) Each player must say whether the number he or she landed on is an odd or even number.

* Make multiple copies of the game board and have more dice available if using with the whole class.

Directions: Help the alien find his way back to the the name of the number on which you landed.

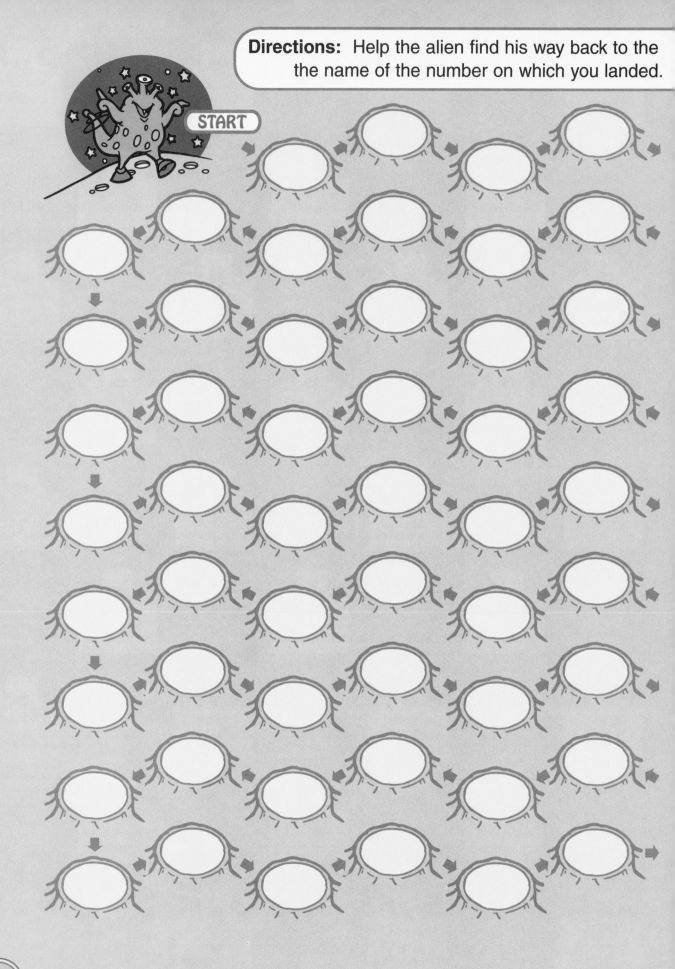

spaceship. Take turns rolling the die. When you move your marker, say
The first one to the spaceship is the winner!

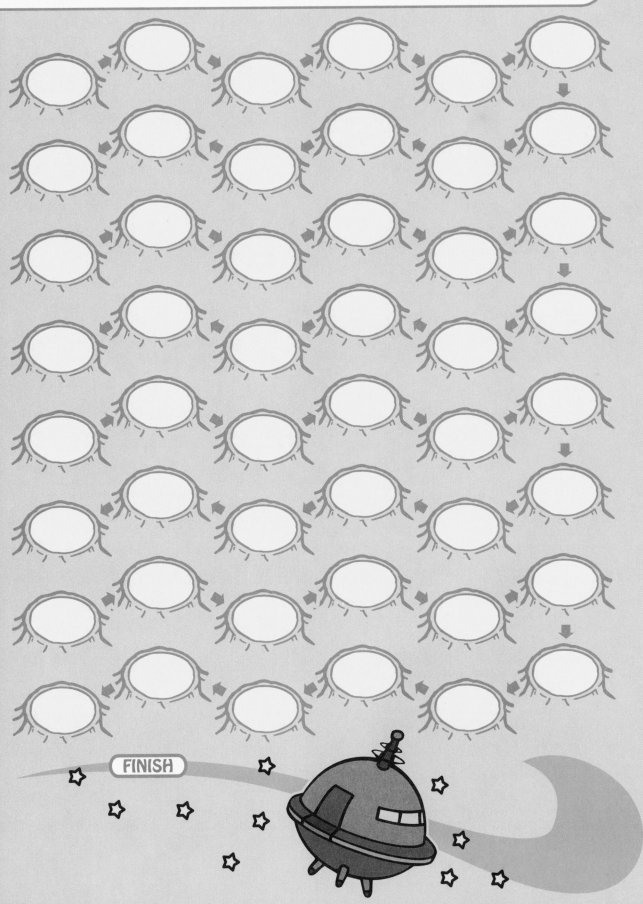

FINISH

42

#3170 Math Literacy Activities

Whose Place Is It Anyway?

 Skill

* identifying numbers
* identifying place value

 Student Grouping

* independent
* partner
* small group
* center

 Materials

* one Number Mat (page 45)
* Number Cards (page 47)

Directions

1. Choose the Number Mat that matches with the level of the students.

2. Lay the Number Mat on a flat surface.

3. Place all Number Cards in a pile mixed up face down.

4. The first player picks the amount of cards the mat can hold. For example, the "Tens" and "Ones" Mat can only hold two cards so the player must choose two cards.

5. The first player must lay the cards on the mat and say the name of the number. Then the first player must say the correct values of the number. For instance, the number 53 would have 5 tens and 3 ones.

6. If the first player says the correct name and correct value, he or she gets a point.

7. The number cards chosen are placed back in the pile mixed up, and the second player gets his or her turn.

8. The game can finish whenever players deem that it is time to end the game.

9. The winning player is the one with the most points.

 Ideas

* Laminate Number Mats and Number Cards for durability.
* Make multiple copies of Number Mats and Number Cards when playing with a whole group.
* Use the numbers and mats for other math lessons.

Number Mats

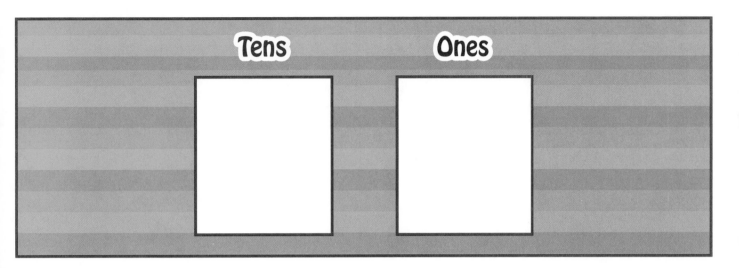

Tens   Ones

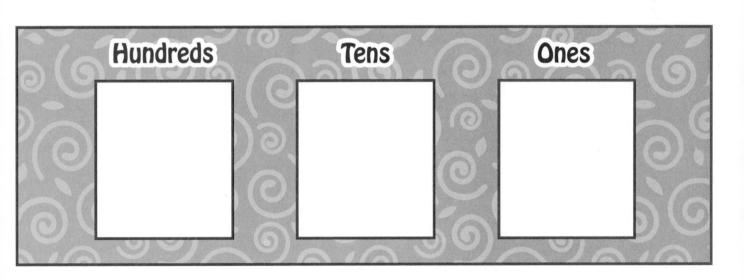

Hundreds   Tens   Ones

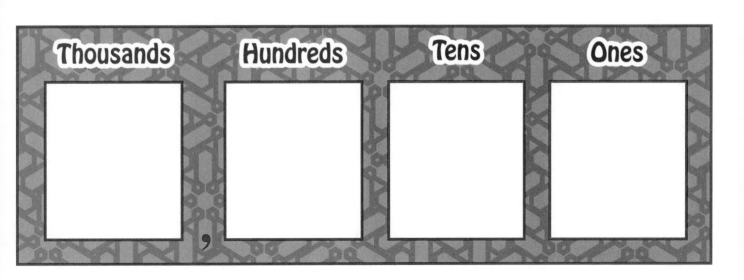

Thousands   Hundreds   Tens   Ones

#3170 Math Literacy Activities

Number Cards

0	0	1	1
2	2	3	3
4	4	5	5
6	6	7	7
8	8	9	9

#3170 Math Literacy Activities

#3170 Math Literacy Activities

©*Teacher Created Resources, Inc.*

Savory Sequences

 Skill

* counting by 10s, 5s, and 2s

 Student Grouping

* independent
* center
* partners
* small group

 Materials

Use the following appropriate board and cards:

* Tasty Tens board (page 51) with matching cards (page 57)
* Fabulous Fives board (page 53) with matching cards (page 57)
* Tantalizing Twos board (page 55) with matching cards (page 57)

 Directions

1. Choose the appropriate board and cards.
2. Lay the board on a flat surface.
3. Mix up the cards.
4. Player 1 chooses a card.
5. Player 1 finds the correct space on the board and lays the card on the space.
6. The next player picks a card and finds the correct space on the board.
7. Play continues until all cards are finished.
8. Have students read the sequence of numbers together.

Ideas

* Laminate the game board and cards for durability.
* After the game is finished, challenge each student to say the sequence without looking at the board.
* To make it more challenging, have students continue the sequence on a separate sheet of paper.
* Have students create a board and more cards that continue the sequences or have them create a new number sequence such as 3s.
* Copy the hundred charts on page 61 for each student. Have each student highlight the number sequences in the chart. For example, he or she can highlight the sequence of 5s in purple. Have students keep the chart handy for reference.

Tasty Tens

Directions: Place the numeral cards in a pile face down. Pick a card and put it in the correct space in order to count by tens.

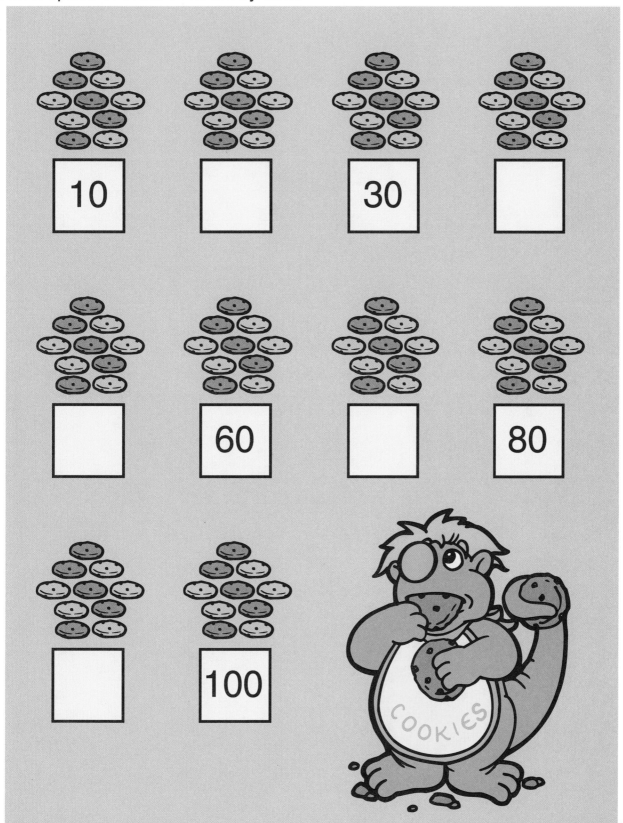

10

30

60

80

100

#3170 Math Literacy Activities

Fabulous Fives

Directions: Place the numeral cards in a pile face down. Pick a card and put it in the correct space in order to count by fives.

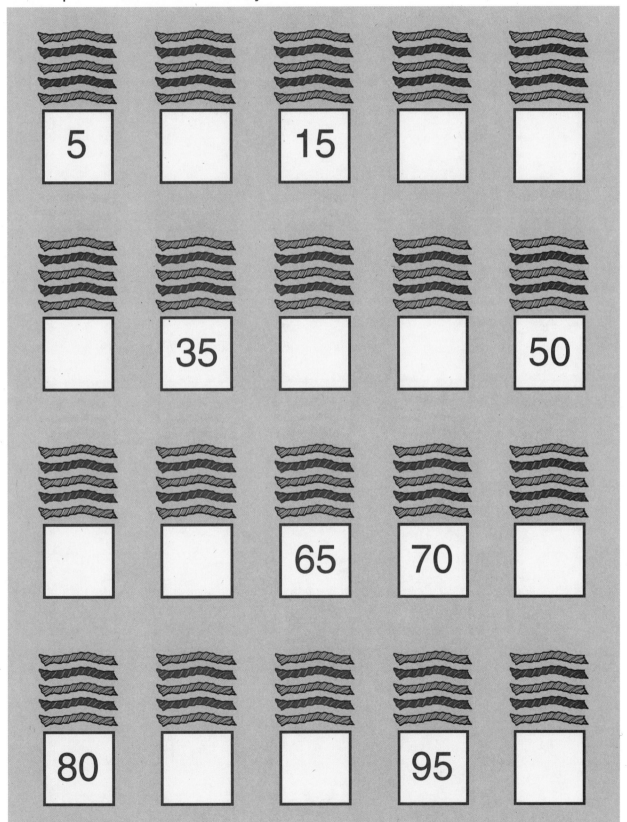

#3170 Math Literacy Activities

©*Teacher Created Resources, Inc.*

Tantalizing Twos

Directions: Place the numeral cards in a pile face down. Pick a card and put it in the correct space in order to count by twos.

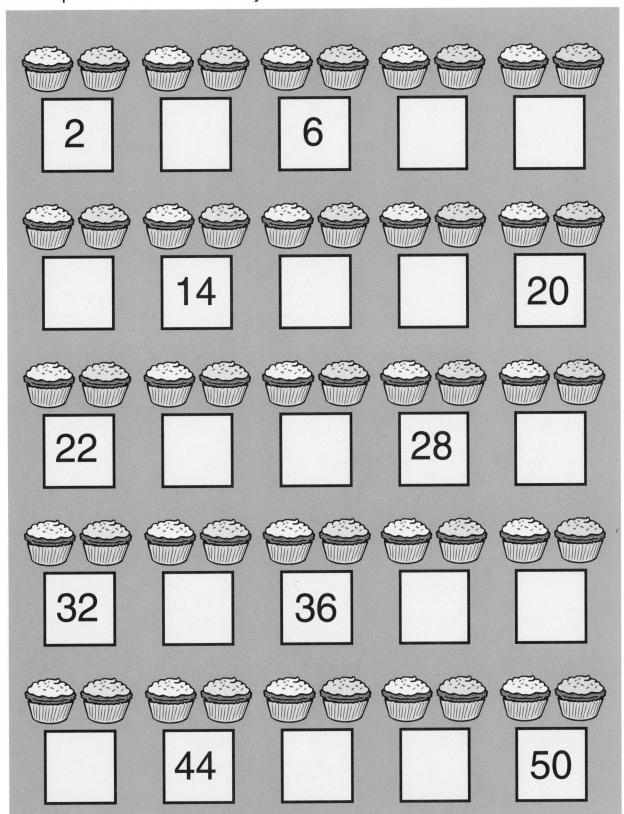

Sequence Cards

Use with page 51.

| 20 | 40 | 50 | 70 | 90 |

Use with page 53.

10	20	25	30	40
45	55	60	75	85
90	100			

Use with page 55.

4	8	10	12	16
18	24	26	30	34
38	40	42	46	48

#3170 Math Literacy Activities

#3170 Math Literacy Activities

Create Your Own Comparison

 ## Skill

* Understanding basic whole number relationships (greater than, less than, and equal to)

 ## Student Grouping

* independent
* partner
* small group
* whole group
* center

 ## Materials

* two copies of the Hundred Chart on page 61 for each student (Have students cut up all number squares prior to the activity.)
* copies of the worksheet on page 60 for each student
* pencils
* glue
* bag for each student

 ## Directions

1. Place all cut-up number squares from the Hundred Chart and place them in a bag.
2. Give each student a worksheet.
3. Each student picks two number squares out of his or her bag.
4. Have the student glue the number squares on the worksheet next to problem number one.
5. The student compares the two numbers and writes in the appropriate sign (<, >, or =).
6. The student continues the process until all problems are completed on the worksheet.
7. Have students' work checked by a teacher or another student.

Ideas

* Copy extra worksheets. Place squares and worksheets in a center.
* If you do not want to make this a cut-and-paste activity as stated above, have each player just write the numbers they chose from his or her bag on the worksheet instead of gluing them.
* Enlarge and laminate the Hundred Chart on page 61 for students to use as a reference.
* Use only numbers 1–25 or 1–50 for students who are having difficulty with this activity.
* If students finish early, have them pull three numbers out of the bag and put them in order, largest to smallest or smallest to largest.

Create Your Comparison

Directions: Choose two numbers from the bag. Place them in the squares. Compare the numbers. Write the appropriate sign (<, >, or =) in the circle between them.

< is less than   **> is greater than**   **= is equal to**

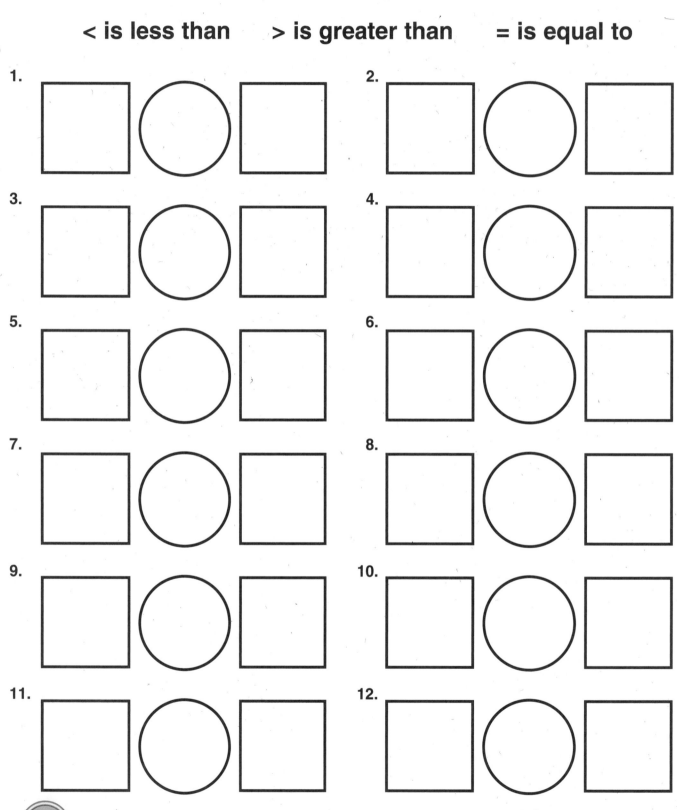

1.

2.

3.

4.

5.

6.

7.

8.

9.

10.

11.

12.

#3170 Math Literacy Activities   ©*Teacher Created Resources, Inc.*

Hundred Chart

1	2	3	4	5	6	7	8	9	10
11	12	13	14	15	16	17	18	19	20
21	22	23	24	25	26	27	28	29	30
31	32	33	34	35	36	37	38	39	40
41	42	43	44	45	46	47	48	49	50
51	52	53	54	55	56	57	58	59	60
61	62	63	64	65	66	67	68	69	70
71	72	73	74	75	76	77	78	79	80
81	82	83	84	85	86	87	88	89	90
91	92	93	94	95	96	97	98	99	100

#3170 Math Literacy Activities

Order in the Zoo!

Skill

✶ using ordinal numbers   ✶ reading ordinal number words

Student Grouping

✶ independent   ✶ small group   ✶ center

Materials

✶ Ordinal Mat (top half of page 65 or both mats on page 65)

✶ Ordinal Cards (page 67 or pages 67 and 69)

✶ Zoo Animal Cards (top of page 71 or all of page 71)

Directions

1. Lay the Ordinal Mat (first–fifth) on a flat surface. (*Note:* If you would like to make the game more challenging, lay the Ordinal Mat [sixth–tenth] on the right of the Ordinal Mat [first–fifth].)

2. Cut apart all cards.

3. Place the pile of Ordinal Cards (first–fifth) face down. (*Note:* If using both Ordinal Mats, place the Ordinal Cards [first–fifth] from page 67 in one pile and the Ordinal Cards [sixth–tenth] from page 69 in another pile.)

4. The first player chooses a card from the pile. (*Note:* If using all Ordinal Cards, then have the player pick one card from each pile.)

5. The first player reads the Ordinal Card (or cards if using both sets).

6. The first player places the Zoo Animals in the correct places on the mat according to the direction of the card (or cards if using both sets).

7. When the first player is finished, the other players check to see if the animals were placed in the correct spaces. If the cards are correctly placed, the player gets one point. If it is not correct, the player does not score any points.

8. The next player continues to repeat the process.

9. The game is finished when all Ordinal Cards are used up.

Ideas

✶ Laminate the mats, problem cards, and animal cards for durability. For center use, place each set of Ordinal Cards and Zoo Animal Cards with the appropriate mat in plastic bags.

✶ For whole class use, copy a mat and the appropriate animal set for each child. The teacher or a designated student can pick an Ordinal Card and read it. The whole class can put the animals in the order on their mats as directed from the card.

Ordinal Mat

Direction: Place the animals in order according to the problem on the card.

first	second	third	fourth	fifth

Ordinal Mat

Direction: Place the animals in order according to the problem on the card.

sixth	seventh	eighth	ninth	tenth

Ordinal Cards (1st–5th)

The hippo is first.
The giraffe is second.
The bear is third.
The kangaroo is fourth.
The turtle is fifth.

The kangaroo is second.
The bear is third.
The giraffe is after the bear.
The hippo is before the kangaroo.
The turtle is after the giraffe.

The kangaroo is first.
The hippo is second.
The giraffe is third.
The turtle is fourth.
The bear is fifth.

The giraffe is fourth.
The turtle is first.
The bear is after the turtle.
The hippo is before the giraffe.
The kangaroo is after the giraffe.

The giraffe is first.
The kangaroo is third.
The hippo is after the giraffe.
The turtle is after the kangaroo.
The bear is after the turtle.

The giraffe is second.
The bear is before the giraffe.
The kangaroo is fourth.
The turtle is after the giraffe.
The hippo is after the kangaroo.

The bear is first.
The kangaroo is fourth.
The giraffe is before the kangaroo.
The hippo is before the giraffe.
The turtle is after the kangaroo.

The hippo is first.
The turtle is fourth.
The giraffe is before the turtle.
The kangaroo is before the giraffe.
The bear is after the turtle.

The bear is third.
The giraffe is after the bear.
The kangaroo is before the bear.
The turtle is before the kangaroo.
The hippo is after the giraffe.

The kangaroo is first.
The bear is third.
The turtle is fourth.
The hippo is before the bear.
The giraffe is after the turtle.

#3170 Math Literacy Activities

The zebra is sixth.
The lion is tenth.
The monkey is eighth.
The elephant is after the monkey.
The tiger is before the monkey.

The tiger is tenth.
The zebra is ninth.
The monkey is two places before the zebra.
The elephant is before the zebra.
The lion is sixth.

The elephant is sixth.
The tiger is tenth.
The monkey is before the tiger.
The zebra is seventh.
The lion is in the middle.

The elephant is ninth.
The tiger is three places before the elephant.
The zebra is after the tiger.
The monkey is eighth.
The lion is after the elephant.

The elephant is eighth.
The zebra is two places after the elephant.
The lion is two places before the elephant.
The tiger is seventh.
The monkey is next to the tenth place.

The zebra is ninth.
The tiger is after the zebra.
The elephant is sixth.
The lion is seventh.
The monkey is after the lion.

The monkey is seventh.
The tiger is sixth.
The zebra is last.
The elephant is eighth.
The lion is before the zebra.

The lion is ninth.
The tiger is sixth.
The monkey is after the lion.
The zebra is eighth.
The elephant is before the zebra.

The lion is sixth.
The monkey is two places after the lion.
The elephant is in between the lion and the monkey.
The tiger is last.
The zebra is after the monkey.

The zebra is ninth.
The tiger is after the zebra.
The lion is eighth.
The elephant is sixth.
The monkey is after the elephant.

Zoo Animal Cards

Use with Ordinal Mat (first–fifth) on the top of page 65.

Use with Ordinal Mat (sixth–tenth) on the bottom of page 65.

#3170 Math Literacy Activities

Time to Go Fish!

 Skill

* identifying time on the hour, half hour, and/or to the minute

 Student Grouping

* partner   * small group   * center

 Materials

* appropriate set of time cards (pages 75–85)

 Directions

1. Choose one of the following ways to play this game depending on ability of students.

   * Time on the Hour Cards
     (pages 75 and 77)

   * Time to the Minute Cards
     (pages 83 and 85)

   * Time on the Half Hour Cards
     (pages 79 and 81)

   * use all sets or two sets of time cards
     (pages 75–85)

2. Mix up the set of cards.

3. Each player draws four cards.

4. Explain that each player needs to match the digital clock time with the face clock. For example, the digital clock showing 2:00 must be matched up with the face clock showing 2:00.

5. Each player should check to see if any matches were made from the four cards that were drawn.

6. Then the first player asks one of the other players for one of his or her matching cards. For example, "John, do you have 3:30?"

7. If the other player answers "yes," he or she must give the matching card to the first player and draw another card. The first player lays down his match on the table. If the other player answers "Time to go fish!", then the first player must draw another card. (*Note:* If there are no cards from which to pull, then just skip to the next player. Also, encourage other players to check to make sure all matches are correct.)

8. Then the second player repeats the same process.

9. The game is finished when one person runs out of cards or all matches have been made.

 Ideas

* Laminate cards for durability.

* If using at a center, a student can independently match the cards.

* For whole-class use, make multiple copies of the sets. Hand out a card to each student. Have each student find the other classmate who has his or her match. Then collect the cards and repeat the process again.

Time on the Hour Cards

Time on the Hour Cards

 1:00

 2:00

 3:00

 4:00

 5:00

 6:00

 7:00

 8:00

 9:00

 10:00

 11:00

 12:00

#3170 Math Literacy Activities

Time on the Half Hour Cards

Time on the Half Hour Cards

 1:30

 2:30

 3:30

 4:30

 5:30

 6:30

 7:30

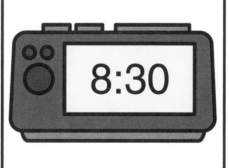 8:30

 9:30

 10:30

 11:30

 12:30

#3170 Math Literacy Activities

82

#3170 Math Literacy Activities

©*Teacher Created Resources, Inc.*

Time to the Minute Cards

#3170 Math Literacy Activities

Time to the Minute Cards

 1:40

 2:35

 3:25

 4:55

 5:50

 6:20

 7:20

 8:05

 9:10

 10:35

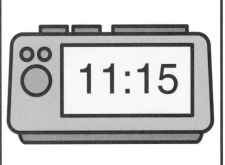 11:15

 12:45

Ice Cream Operations

 Skill

✻ adds, subtracts, or multiplies whole numbers

 Student Grouping

✻ independent

✻ partner

✻ center

 Materials

✻ Ice Cream Cone Board (page 89)

✻ Addition Ice Cream (page 91), Subtraction Ice Cream (page 93), or Multiplication Ice Cream (page 95) precut

 Directions

1. Choose one of the following "ice cream" cards to play:

   ✻ Addition Ice Cream (page 91)

   ✻ Subtraction Ice Cream (page 93)

   ✻ Multiplication Ice Cream (page 95)

2. Lay the Ice Cream Cone Board on a flat surface.

3. Place the set of Ice Cream cards face down.

4. Pick one of the cards and place it on the correct cone. The number on the cone should be the answer to the math problem on the ice cream.

5. The process continues until all ice cream cards are finished.

Ideas

✻ Laminate board and ice cream cards. Store ice cream cards in small, plastic bags.

✻ Keep time to see how fast each individual can solve the board.

✻ Have students create their own "ice cream" cards by cutting from construction paper more circular shapes that would match the size of the Ice Cream Cone Board. Then have students write other math problems on the circular pieces of paper. They can play the activity with their own "ice cream" pieces or have partners play their pieces on the board. Make sure they have an "ice cream" problem for each of the cones and designate which operation (addition, subtraction, or multiplication) you want students to use.

Ice Cream Cone Board

Directions: Match the problem on the ice cream to the correct answer on the cone.

#3170 Math Literacy Activities

Addition Ice Cream

4
+ 3
___

5
+ 1
___

6
+ 2
___

3
+ 6
___

3
+ 2
___

8
+ 2
___

6
+ 5
___

1
+ 3
___

9
+ 3
___

0
+ 2
___

1
+ 2
___

1
+ 0
___

#3170 Math Literacy Activities

Subtraction Ice Cream

8
− 1
_____

6
− 4
_____

9
− 4
_____

7
− 3
_____

10
− 2
_____

12
− 0
_____

6
− 5
_____

9
− 3
_____

8
− 5
_____

11
− 2
_____

12
− 1
_____

12
− 2
_____

#3170 Math Literacy Activities

Multiplication Ice Cream

7
x 1
___

1
x 2
___

5
x 1
___

2
x 2
___

4
x 2
___

6
x 2
___

3
x 3
___

1
x 1
___

2
x 3
___

11
x 1
___

5
x 2
___

3
x 1
___

#3170 Math Literacy Activities

Pieces of Pizza

 Skill

* understand commonly used fractions

 Student Grouping

* independent
* partner
* center

 Materials

* Pizza and Fraction Cards (pages 99 and 101)

 Directions

1. Mix up the cards and face them down individually on a flat surface.

2. Player 1 chooses two cards.

3. If the fraction and picture match, Player 1 keeps the pair and Player 1 gets another turn. If the fraction and picture do not match, the cards are then placed face down and Player 2 takes his or her turn. The goal is to find the picture that matches with each fraction.

4. The activity continues until all matches have been made.

Ideas

* Encourage students to remember where cards are placed.

* Laminate cards for durability. Store each set in a small, plastic bag.

* Copy a set of Pizza and Fraction Cards for each student and have students make fraction posters by gluing the matches together. Students can use the poster as a reference.

* Use Pizza and Fraction Cards to support your math lesson on fractions.

Pizza and Fraction Cards

$$\frac{1}{1} = 1$$

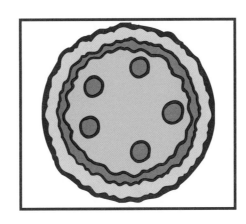

$$\frac{1}{2}$$

$$\frac{1}{3}$$

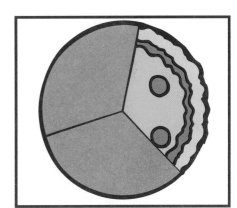

$$\frac{1}{4}$$

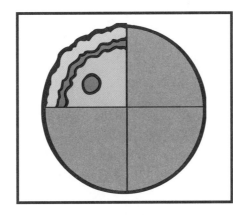

$$\frac{2}{3}$$

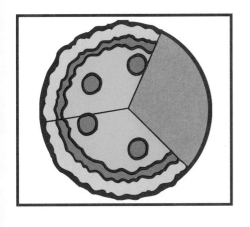

$$\frac{3}{4}$$

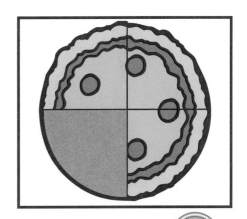

#3170 Math Literacy Activities

Pizza and Fraction Cards

$$\frac{1}{5}$$

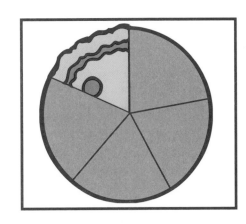

$$\frac{4}{5}$$

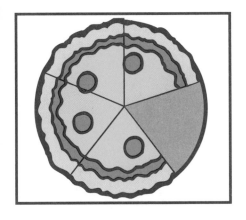

$$\frac{5}{6}$$

$$\frac{6}{7}$$

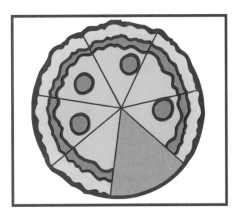

$$\frac{7}{8}$$

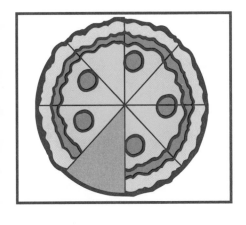

$$\frac{8}{9}$$

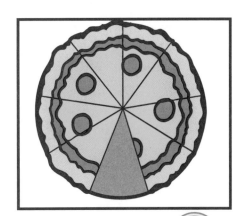

#3170 Math Literacy Activities

Help Henry!

 Skill

* solving real-world problems involving addition, subtraction, multiplication, and time
* developing fluency in number computation

 **Student Grouping**

* independent   * whole group   * small group   * partner   * center

 Materials

* Help Henry! Game Board (page 105)
* appropriate set of word problem cards precut (pages 107–121)
* appropriate matching Answer Card (pages 123–129)
* blank paper for solving problems

* playing marker for each student
* pencils

 Directions

1. Set the word problem cards face down in a pile. (*Note:* Make sure to match the word problem cards with your students' levels.)

2. Place the playing markers on the game board on "START." (*Note:* For whole-group use, copy a game board for each student. Have the student monitor his or her own game board.)

3. Player 1 picks a word problem card and reads it to all players. (*Note:* If the student is at a beginning reading level, the teacher or a more fluent reader can help the student read the card.) Then all players try to solve the problem. (*Note:* Encourage students to use drawings or manipulatives to solve their problems, when necessary. For time word problems, have mini-clocks available for students to use.)

4. Then Player 1 reads the correct answer from the Answer Card. (*Note:* When looking for answers on the Answer Card, tell students to look for the object that matches the word problem.) All students with the correct answer move forward one space.

5. Player 2 picks a word problem card and reads it to all players. Then all players try to solve the problem.

6. Then Player 2 reads the correct answer from the Answer Card. All students with the correct answer move forward one space. The process continues until a player (or players) reaches "FINISH."

Ideas

* Use the word problem cards to supplement your math lesson.
* Laminate the game board, each set of word problem cards, and matching answer card. Store each set of word problem cards and answer cards in a plastic bag.
* Discuss with students how they solved their problems. Encourage those who did not get the correct answers to find out what they did wrong. Tell students to watch for key words such as "in all" or "have left."
* When playing with the whole group, break students into teams.

Help Henry! Game Board

Directions: Help Henry find his way home by solving the word problems on the cards.

START

FINISH

#3170 Math Literacy Activities

Addition Word Problems

(Single Digit)

Sue counted 8 red roses and 6 white roses in the garden. How many roses did Sue find in all?

Dan ate 3 apples for breakfast. He ate 4 more for snack. How many apples did he eat in all?

My mom bought 4 pizzas. My dad bought 5 pizzas. How many pizzas did they buy in all?

Joe saw 9 butterflies. Jack saw 3 butterflies. How many butterflies did they see in all?

Alex made 7 books using crayons and 4 books using markers. How many books did he make in all?

My aunt baked 5 hams. My grandpa baked 5 hams. How many hams did they bake in all?

Buster barked at the mail person 5 times and 3 times at a boy riding a bike. How many times did Buster bark?

Jenny made 8 kites. Tammy made 9 kites. How many kites did they make in all?

On the school bus there were 6 boys and 5 girls. How many children were there on the school bus?

Steve picked up 2 small sticks and 7 large sticks. How many sticks did he pick up in all?

Hector ate 6 chips and 2 bowls of chili. How many things did Hector eat in all?

Sheba ate 3 bones for breakfast and 9 for lunch. How many bones did Sheba eat in all?

#3170 Math Literacy Activities

Addition Word Problems

(Double-Digit Without Regrouping)

Charlie has 63 coins in his piggy bank. Sondra has 21 coins in her piggy bank. How many coins do they have in all?

The class made 55 blueberry pancakes and 41 buttermilk pancakes. How many pancakes did they make in all?

Patty went on the camel ride 41 times. Rachel went on the camel ride 18 times. How many times did the girls ride the camel in all?

Dean fed the monkey 31 peanuts. Tom fed the monkey 24 peanuts. How many peanuts did the monkey eat in all?

Nate has 26 toy cars. David has 13 more toy cars than Nate. How many toy cars does David have?

A mouse ate 44 pieces of cheese Sunday. On Monday he ate 20 pieces of cheese. How many pieces on cheese did he eat altogether on Sunday and Monday?

At the morning show, the kangaroo jumped 70 feet. During the evening show, the kangaroo jumped 25 feet. How far did the kangaroo jump in all?

 Fred bought 10 tickets. A friend gave him 15 more. How many tickets does Fred have in all?

 Mr. Hill caught 27 fish in the morning and 42 fish in the evening. How many fish did he catch in all?

Sheri made 14 baskets in the first game and 35 baskets in the second game. How many baskets did Sheri make in all?

Doug has a necktie with 51 red dots and 27 blue dots. How many dots on his tie did Doug have in all?

Marsha had 22 stamps in her collection. Her sister gave her 25 more. How many stamps does Marsha have in all?

Addition Word Problems

(Double Digits With Regrouping)

Amy caught 38 insects in a net and 54 insects in a box. How many insects did Amy catch in all?

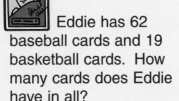 Eddie has 62 baseball cards and 19 basketball cards. How many cards does Eddie have in all?

Betty cooked 27 cookies. Her friend baked 46 cookies. How many cookies did they bake in all?

 At the circus, Kenny saw 17 tigers and 27 monkeys. How many animals did he see in all?

At the beach, Mandy counted 28 round seashells and 36 pointed seashells. How many seashells did she count in all?

Jason saw 56 stars on Monday and 26 stars on Tuesday. How many stars did he see altogether on Monday and Tuesday?

Nick drove his car 47 miles on Friday and 25 miles on Sunday. How many miles did Nick drive in all?

Beth has 28 teddy bears. Her grandma gave her 12 more. How many teddy bears does Beth have now?

Mike has 34 toy dinosaurs. He bought 17 more. How many toy dinosaurs does Mike have now?

 Kim has 42 pencils. She bought 18 more. How many pencils does she have now?

 Ron hit 36 golf balls in the morning and then hit another 35 golf balls in the afternoon? How many golf balls did he hit in all?

Kris has 19 marbles in his bag. His friend gave him 24 more to put in the bag. How many marbles does Kris have now?

#3170 Math Literacy Activities

#3170 Math Literacy Activities   ©*Teacher Created Resources, Inc.*

Subtraction Word Problems

(Single Digit)

 Jim had 9 oranges. He ate 2. How many are left?

 Deb had 5 dolls. Now she only has 2. How many dolls did she lose?

 Hope picked 7 strawberries. John ate 4 of them. How many does Hope have left?

 Jake had 8 candy bars. His friend ate 2 of them. How many candy bars does Jake have left?

 Lisa has a cat with 6 fleas. If 3 jumped off, how many fleas are left?

 Ken found 4 snails in the garden. He picked up 2 of them. How many snails are left in the garden?

 Cory planted 9 seeds. Only 5 grew. How many seeds did not grow?

 Bob bought 8 doughnuts. He ate 3 of them. How many doughnuts does Bob have left?

 Wilbur had 5 spiders. 1 spider ran away. How many spiders does Wilbur have now?

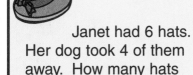 Janet had 6 hats. Her dog took 4 of them away. How many hats does Janet have left?

Jackie had 7 basketballs. 6 of them are flat. How many basketballs still bounce?

Zach had 9 yo-yos. 7 of them broke. How many yo-yos does Zach have left?

Subtraction Word Problems

(Double Digits Without Regrouping)

Ted found 36 socks. He took 14 of them to the laundry room. How many socks does he still have in his room?

Andy has 75 pieces of candy. He gives 35 to Emily. How many pieces of candy does Andy have left?

Rosa baked 30 cupcakes for her class. Her dog ate 20 of the cupcakes. How many cupcakes does Rosa have left?

Karen invited 99 people to the party. Only 30 came. How many people did not come to the party?

Sharon had 64 chocolate covered candies in the jar. Now there are only 22 chocolate covered candies in the jar. How many chocolate covered candies did Sharon eat?

Pam has 32 rings. Jan has 21 fewer rings than Pam. How many rings does Jan have?

Mary saw 43 turtles. Lori saw 10 fewer turtles than Mary. How many turtles did Lori see?

Ms. Jones put 25 vegetables into her pot of soup. If 13 of them were onions, how many were not onions?

Mr. Smith picked 58 heads of lettuce. He gave his friends 26 heads of lettuce. How many heads of lettuce does Mr. Smith have left?

Matt made 39 peanut butter and jelly sandwiches. His friends ate 12 of them. How many sandwiches does Matt have left?

Judy had 85 dresses. She gave 53 of them away. How many dresses does she have left?

Norma bought 28 gallons of ice cream for a party. The children ate 13 gallons. How many gallons are left?

Subtraction Word Problems

(Double Digits With Regrouping)

Daniel scored 43 points in a card game. Scott scored 27 points. What is the difference in points?

Jill counted 83 ants near an ant hill. Jason counted 65. What is the difference in the ants counted?

Lupe needs 41 candles. There are only 23 candles. How many more candles does Lupe need?

Jerry unpacked 67 Christmas lights. If 19 were broken, how many lights were not broken?

There were 71 birds in the bird show. Monica saw only 46 of the birds. How many birds did Monica not see?

The zookeeper had 86 crickets in a jar. She gave the tortoise 57 of the crickets. How many crickets does the zookeeper have left?

Mark has 53 pairs of shoes. Clark has 24 pairs of shoes. How many more pairs of shoes does Mark have than Clark?

At the first baseball game of the season, 94 fans came to watch. During the second game, there were 76 fans. How many fewer fans came to watch the second game?

Tom had shot an arrow and received 32 points. He shot it again and received 18 points. What is the difference in points?

Luke had 38 tires. 29 of them were flat. How many tires were not flat?

Josh saw 44 paw prints. Mary saw 27 fewer paw prints than Josh. How many paw prints did Mary see?

Ms. Thomas had 48 pencils and 19 calculators. How many more pencils does she have than calculators?

Multiplication Word Problems

(Single Digit)

Gary has 2 wheels on each of the 3 bikes. How many wheels does Gary have altogether?

Sophie has 4 birds. Each bird has 2 legs. How many bird legs are there in all?

Tim has 5 hats in 7 boxes. How many hats are there in all?

Jane has 6 pieces of cake on each of the 4 trays. How many pieces of cake are there in all?

Mel played 8 rounds of jacks. She won 5 jacks in each round. How many jacks did Mel win altogether?

Dee saw 3 necklaces on each of the 9 shelves. She bought all the necklaces on those shelves. How many necklaces did Dee buy altogether?

James has 4 brothers. He has to buy 4 presents for each of his brothers. How many presents does James have to buy in all?

Becky sewed 9 buttons on 5 shirts. How many buttons did she sew altogether?

Nicole has 3 paint brushes in each of 7 cans. How many paint brushes does Nicole have altogether?

Max has 5 pockets. He has 5 marbles in each pocket. How many marbles does Max have altogether?

Don had 9 baskets. There were 6 balls in each basket. How many balls were there altogether?

Janet placed 3 candy bars in each of the 4 bags. How many candy bars did she place in the bags altogether?

#3170 Math Literacy Activities

©*Teacher Created Resources, Inc.*

Time Word Problems

Steve went to a Saturday night movie at 7:30 P.M. He arrived home 3 hours later. What time did Steve get home?

Dana started soccer practice at 2:30 P.M. and finished 15 minutes later. What time did Dana finish?

Bob practices the guitar every day for 1/2 an hour. If Bob starts his practice at 6:00 P.M., at what time will he finish?

Loren comes home from work at 5:00 P.M. If she eats dinner two hours later, when does Loren eat dinner?

Carol's party started at 1:00 P.M. and ended at 5:00 P.M. How many hours was the party?

The baby fell asleep at 9:00 A.M. and napped for 1 hour. What time did the baby wake up?

Scott went to the park at 3:30 P.M. He played for 2 hours. What time did Scott finish playing?

Recess begins at 10:30 A.M. and ends at 11:00 A.M. How long is recess?

Lunch starts at 12:30 P.M. and ends at 1:15 P.M. How long is lunch?

Mrs. White teaches math from 9:00 A.M. to 10:30 A.M. How much time is spent in math class?

School starts at 8:00 A.M. School is over at 3:00 P.M. How many hours are children at school?

Band practice is from 2:00 P.M. to 3:30 P.M. How long is band practice?

Answer Cards

Use with problems on page 109.

Answer Card
(Addition–Double Digit Without Regrouping)

  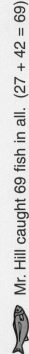

Charlie and Sondra have 84 coins in all. (63 + 21 = 84)

The class made 96 pancakes in all. (55 + 41 = 96)

Patty and Rachel rode the camel 59 times in all. (41 + 18 = 59)

The monkey ate 55 peanuts in all. (31 + 24 = 55)

David has 39 toy cars. (26 + 13 = 39)

The mouse ate 64 pieces of cheese altogether. (44 + 20 = 64)

The kangaroo jumped 95 feet. (70 + 25 = 95)

Fred has 25 tickets in all. (10 + 15 = 25)

Mr. Hill caught 69 fish in all. (27 + 42 = 69)

Sheri made 49 baskets in all. (14 + 35 = 49)

Doug has 78 dots in all. (51 + 27 = 78)

Marsha has 47 stamps in all. (22 + 25 = 47)

Use with problems on page 107.

Answer Card
(Addition–Single Digit)

Sue found 14 roses in all. (8 + 6 = 14)

Dan ate 7 apples in all. (3 + 4 = 7)

Mom and dad bought 9 pizzas in all. (5 + 4 = 9)

Joe and Jack saw 12 butterflies in all. (9 + 3 = 12)

Alex made 11 books in all. (7 + 4 = 11)

My aunt and grandpa baked 10 hams in all. (5 + 5 = 10)

Buster barked 8 times. (5 + 3 = 8)

Jenny and Tammy made 17 kites in all. (8 + 9 = 17)

There were 11 children on the bus. (6 + 5 = 11)

Steve picked up 9 sticks in all. (2 + 7 = 9)

Hector ate 8 things in all. (6 + 2 = 8)

Sheba ate 12 bones in all. (3 + 9 = 12)

Answer Cards

Use with problems on page 113.

Answer Card
(Subtraction–Single Digit)

 Jim has 7 oranges left. $(9 - 2 = 7)$

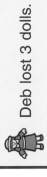 Deb lost 3 dolls. $(5 - 2 = 3)$

 Hope has 3 strawberries left. $(7 - 4 = 3)$

 Jake has 6 candy bars left. $(8 - 2 = 6)$

 Lisa's cat has 3 fleas left. $(6 - 3 = 3)$

 There are 2 snails left in the garden. $(4 - 2 = 2)$

 There are 4 seeds that did not grow. $(9 - 5 = 4)$

 Bob has 5 doughnuts left. $(8 - 3 = 5)$

 Wilbur has 4 spiders now. $(5 - 1 = 4)$

Janet has 2 hats left. $(6 - 4 = 2)$

Jackie has 1 basketball that still bounces. $(7 - 6 = 1)$

Zach has 2 yo-yos left. $(9 - 7 = 2)$

Use with problems on page 111.

Answer Card
(Addition–Double Digit With Regrouping)

 Amy caught 92 insects in all. $(38 + 54 = 92)$

 Eddie has 81 cards in all. $(62 + 19 = 81)$

Betty and her friend baked 73 cookies in all. $(27 + 46 = 73)$

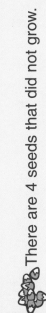 Kenny saw 44 animals in all. $(17 + 27 = 44)$

Mandy counted 64 seashells in all. $(28 + 36 = 64)$

Jason saw 82 stars altogether. $(56 + 26 = 82)$

 Nick drove 72 miles altogether. $(47 + 25 = 72)$

 Beth has 40 teddy bears now. $(28 + 12 = 40)$

 Mike has 51 toy dinosaurs now. $(34 + 17 = 51)$

 Kim has 60 pencils now. $(42 + 18 = 60)$

 Ron hit 71 golf balls in all. $(36 + 35 = 71)$

   Kris has 43 marbles in his bag now. $(19 + 24 = 43)$

#3170 Math Literacy Activities

#3170 Math Literacy Activities

©Teacher Created Resources, Inc.

Use with problems on page 117.

Answer Card
(Subtraction—Double Digits With Regrouping)

 The difference in points is 16 points. (43 − 27 = 16)

 The difference in ants is 18. (83 − 65 = 18)

 Lupe needs 18 more candles. (41 − 23 = 18)

 48 Christmas lights were not broken. (67 − 19 = 48)

 Monica did not see 25 birds. (71 − 46 = 25)

 The zookeeper has 29 crickets left. (86 − 57 = 29)

 Mark has 29 more pairs of shoes. (53 − 24 = 29)

 18 fewer fans came to the second game. (94 − 76 = 18)

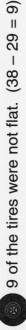 The difference is 14 points. (32 − 18 = 14)

 9 of the tires were not flat. (38 − 29 = 9)

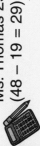 Mary saw 17 paw prints. (44 − 27 = 17)

Ms. Thomas 29 more pencils than calculators. (48 − 19 = 29)

Use with problems on page 115.

Answer Card
(Subtraction—Double Digits Without Regrouping)

 Ted has 22 socks still in his room. (36 − 14 = 22)

 Andy has 40 pieces of candy left. (75 − 35 = 40)

 Rosa has 10 cupcakes left. (30 − 20 = 10)

 69 people did not come to the party. (99 − 30 = 69)

 Sharon ate 42 chocolate covered candies. (64 − 22 = 42)

 Jan has 11 rings. (32 − 21 = 11)

 Lori saw 33 turtles. (43 − 10 = 33)

 12 of the vegetables were not onions. (25 − 13 = 12)

 Mr. Smith has 32 heads of lettuce left. (58 − 26 = 32)

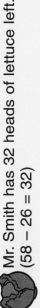 Matt has 27 sandwiches left. (39 − 12 = 27)

 Judy has 32 dresses left. (85 − 53 = 32)

 15 gallons of ice cream are left. (28 − 13 = 15)

Answer Cards

Use with problems on page 121.

Answer Card
(Time)

 Steve got home at 10:30 P.M.

 Dana finished at 2:45 P.M.

 Bob will finish at 6:30 P.M.

 Loren eats dinner at 7:00 P.M.

 Carol's party was 4 hours long.

 The baby woke up at 10:00 A.M.

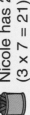 Scott finished playing at 5:30 P.M.

 Recess is 1/2 an hour or 30 minutes long.

 Lunch is 45 minutes.

Math class is 1 1/2 hours long.

 The children are at school for 7 hours.

Band practice is 1 1/2 hours.

Use with problems on page 119.

Answer Card
(Multiplication–Single Digit)

 Gary has 6 wheels in all. (2 x 3 = 6)

 There are 8 bird legs in all. (4 x 2 = 8)

 There are 35 hats in the boxes. (5 x 7 = 35)

 There are 24 pieces of cake in all. (6 x 4 = 24)

 Mel won 40 jacks altogether. (8 x 5 = 40)

 Dee bought 27 necklaces altogether. (3 x 9 = 27)

 James has to buy 16 presents in all. (4 x 4 = 16)

 Becky sewed on 45 buttons altogether. (9 x 5 = 45)

 Nicole has 21 paint brushes altogether. (3 x 7 = 21)

 Max has 25 marbles altogether. (5 x 5 = 25)

 There were 54 balls altogether. (9 x 6 = 54)

There were 12 candy bars altogether. (3 x 4 = 12)

#3170 Math Literacy Activities

 ## Skill

* understanding processes for counting money

 ## Student Grouping

* independent
* partners
* small group
* large group (*Note:* Copy more money and Pocket Mats to have enough for large group.)

 ## Materials

* Pocket Mats (pages 133 and 135)
* appropriate set of Toys For Sale Cards (pages 137–141)
* plastic coin money and dollar bills (*Note:* If you do not have these, then use the money on pages 143–149.)

Directions

1. Choose one of the following sets of Toys For Sale Cards depending on the level of your students: toys under 25¢, toys under $1.00, or toys over a $1.00.
2. Give each student a Pocket Mat.
3. Place a pile of coins (and bills if appropriate) in front of each student.
4. Place the appropriate set of Toys For Sale Cards in a pile.
5. Pick one Toys For Sale Card and show the card to the students.
6. Tell students that they are going to buy the toy and that they must place the correct amount of money in their "pockets" to purchase the toy. Students then place the correct amount of money on their Pocket Mats. Check to see if the correct amount of money was placed on the mats or have students check each other's mats. Encourage students to discuss how they figured their amounts.
7. Continue until all cards are finished.

Ideas

* Laminate Pocket Mats, Toys For Sale Cards, and the paper money for durability.
* For children who need practice identifying coins, place a pile of coins in front of each student. Then ask them to place a certain coin in their "pocket." For example, "Place a nickel in your pocket."
* Have students give each other oral word problems and solve them using their money and Pocket Mats. For instance, one student could say, "John has 1 nickel and 2 dimes in his pocket. How much money does he have?"
* For a challenge, give students a certain amount of money to place in their "pockets." Then show them a Toy For Sale Card. Tell students that they will be purchasing the toy. Students then give you the money and must count out the correct change from a coin pile to place back in their "pockets."

#3170 Math Literacy Activities

Pocket Mats

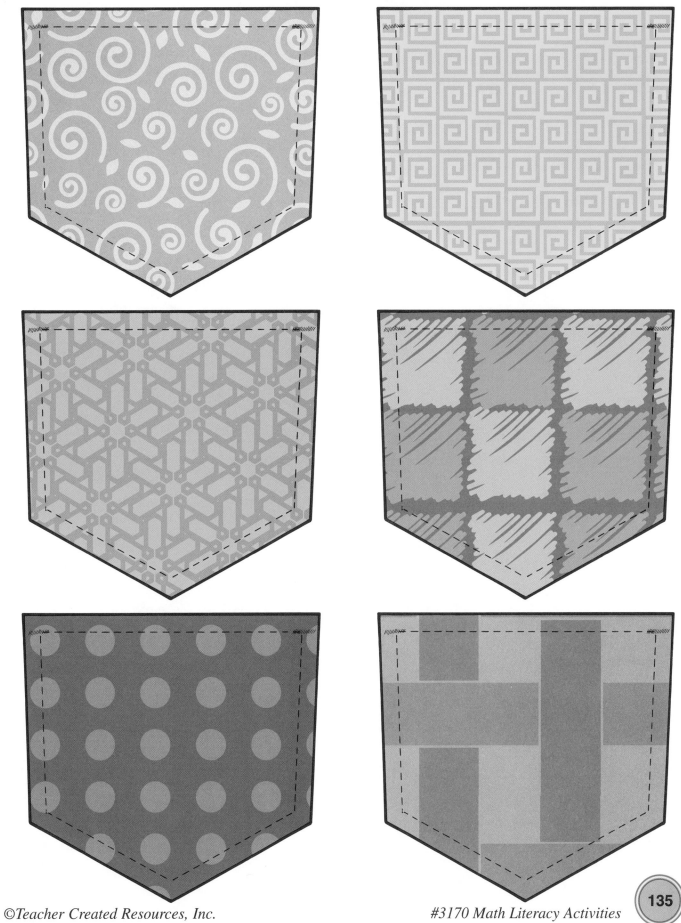

Toys For Sale Cards

(25¢ and Under)

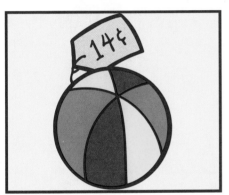  

#3170 Math Literacy Activities

#3170 Math Literacy Activities

Toys For Sale Cards

(Under $1.00)

#3170 Math Literacy Activities

Toys For Sale Cards

(Over $1.00)

 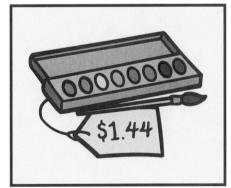 

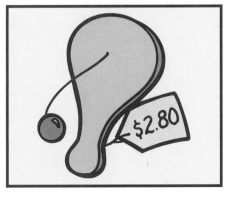  

Money (Coins)

Money (Coins)

Money (Bills)

#3170 Math Literacy Activities

#3170 Math Literacy Activities

©*Teacher Created Resources, Inc.*

Money (Bills)

#3170 Math Literacy Activities

Brain Knockers

Skill

* reads and interprets simple charts and graphs (picture graph, bar graph, or tally chart)

Student Grouping

* independent
* partners
* small group
* large group (make multiple color copies of the chart or graph for students to share)

Materials

* one graph or chart (Choose from pages 153–161. The back of the chart has the answers.)
* pencils
* paper

Directions

1. Pick one graph.
2. Have students study and discuss the graph before answering the questions.
3. Have students answer the questions on the bottom of the chart or graph.
4. Have students look on the back of each graph or chart page to check their answers or read the answers aloud.
5. Have students discuss how they arrived at their answers.

Ideas

* Laminate each graph for durability, especially if using in a center.
* Make sure students have knowledge of tally marks before distributing the tally chart.
* Have students create more questions for each graph.
* Have students select one type of chart or graph. Then have students create their own using the chart or graph as a model.
* Make addition problems from the graphs and chart. For example, 9 dogs + 10 cats = 19.

OCTOBER

Sunday	Monday	Tuesday	Wednesday	Thursday	Friday	Saturday
		1	2	3	4	5
6	7	8	9	10	11	12
13	14	15	16	17	18	19
20	21	22	23	24	25	26
27	28	29	30	31		

Brain Knockers

1. What is the name of the month?

2. How many days are in this month?

3. What day of the week is the 1st?

4. What day of the week is the 21st?

5. How many Saturdays are in October?

Answers

1. October
2. 31
3. Tuesday
4. Monday
5. 4

PERFECT PETS

Ms. Black said that she has a dog. A dog is her favorite pet.
Ms. Black has 25 students in her class. She asked each student what
was his or her favorite pet. This picture graph shows what each
student said.

Favorite Pets

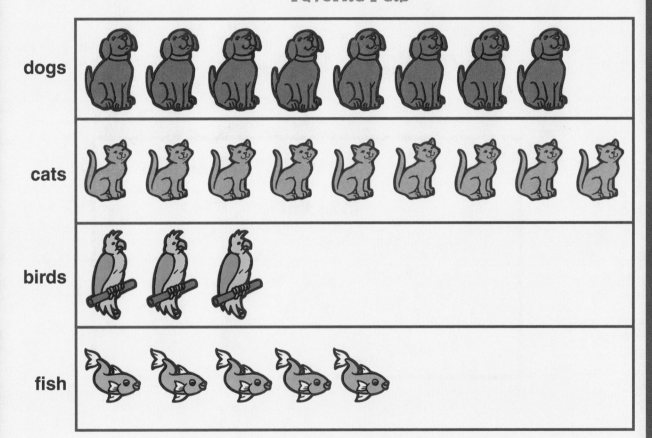

Brain Knockers

1. How many students chose birds as their favorite pet?

2. How many students chose fish as their favorite pet?

3. Which pet had the most votes?

Answers

1. 3
2. 5
3. cat

SMASHING SUBJECTS

The students in Mr. Wood's class took a vote to find out what subject was liked the most by class members. Mr. Wood kept a record of the votes for each subject on a tally chart.

Our Favorite Subjects	
Subject	**Tally of Votes**
math	|||
reading and writing	||||
art	||||
science	|||| |
music	||
physical education	||||

Brain Knockers

1. Which subject was liked the most?

2. Which two subjects had the same number of votes?

3. How many students liked math?

Answers

1. science

2. art and physical education

3. 3

DELICIOUS DESSERTS

Mr. Adams asked his class, "What dessert do you like best?" This bar graph shows how his class voted.

A bar graph titled with DESSERTS on the vertical axis and STUDENTS on the horizontal axis (1 to 10).

Dessert	Votes
Candy	8
Ice Cream	7
Popcorn	0
Cake	3
Cookies	7

Brain Knockers

1. **Which dessert got the most votes?**

2. **Which desserts got the same number of votes?**

3. **Which dessert got the least votes? Why?**

Answers

1. candy

2. ice cream and cookies

3. popcorn—Answers will vary.

CLASS AND COLOR

Mrs. Hill said that her favorite color was green. She said, "All the rooms in my house are green." "What is your favorite color?" she asked.

Here are the favorite colors of the students in her class.

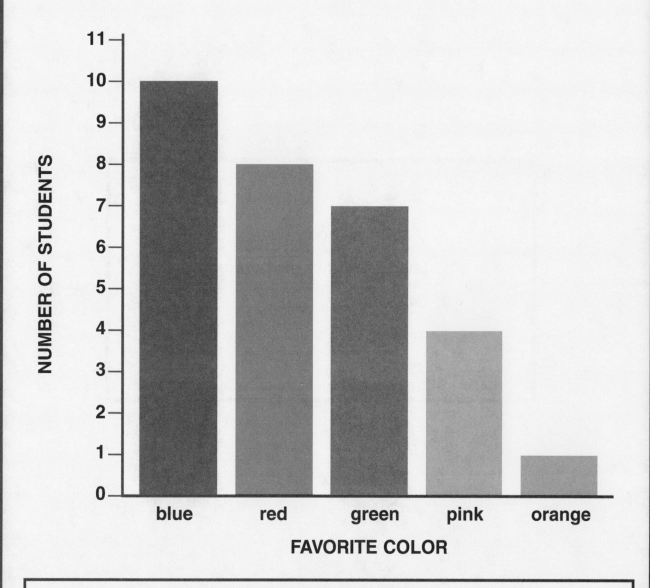

Brain Knockers

1. What does this graph show?

2. What color do the students like most?

3. What color do the students like the least?

Answers

1. favorite colors of the students

2. blue

3. orange

Creepy and Crawly

Skill

* understanding process for measuring length using standard units (inch and centimeter)

Student Grouping

* independent
* small group
* partners
* large group (Place students in partner groups.)

Materials

* one set of precut Creepy and Crawly Cards (pages 165–169)
* rulers (Use rulers on page 173 and 175 if you do not have access to rulers.)
* one answer card (page 171)
* paper
* pencils

Directions

1. Hand out paper, pencils, and rulers to students.
2. Choose one unit of measurement—inches or centimeters—or both depending on the level of your students. Remind the students to use the correct side of the ruler to measure. If students are at an introductory level of measurement, try using paper clips as a unit of measurement first.
3. Place the Creepy and Crawly Cards in a basket and have students pull one bug out of the basket.
4. Have students measure the bug on the card.
5. Have students record the name of the creepy and crawly thing and the measurement on the piece of paper. For example, "fly = 1 inch." (*Note:* For some students, you may want to challenge them to measure to the nearest centimeter.) After they finish one bug, tell them to switch with another student's bug. Tell them that there are 24 creepy and crawly things that they need to measure.
6. After all bugs are measured, have students independently check their answers with the Answer Card or have someone read the answers from the Answer Card to the group.

Ideas

* Laminate bug cards and rulers, especially when using in a center.
* Teach your students different ways to record the measurements: the abbreviations for inch (in.) and centimeter (cm) or the symbol for inch (").
* Have students write an estimation before they actually measure the crawly things on the cards. Then have them compare to see if their estimations were right or not.
* Have students record the measurements in full sentences. For example, "The dragonfly is 3 inches long."

Creepy and Crawly Cards

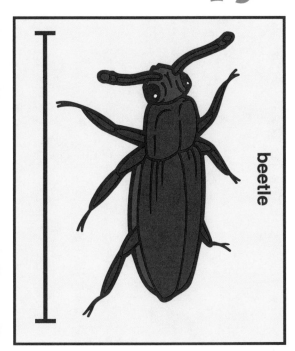

beetle

lady bug

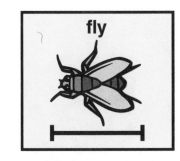

fly

flea

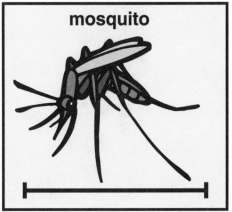

mosquito

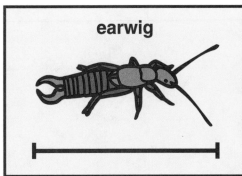

earwig

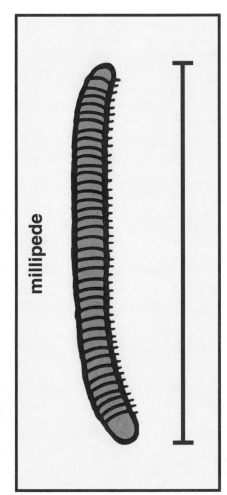

millipede

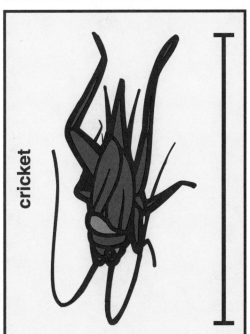

cricket

grasshopper

#3170 Math Literacy Activities

Creepy and Crawly Cards

cockroach

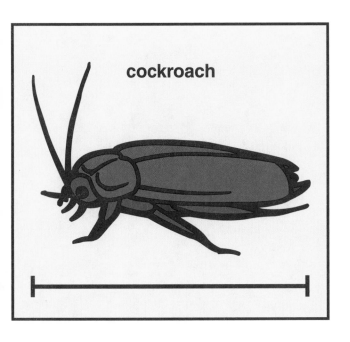

dragonfly

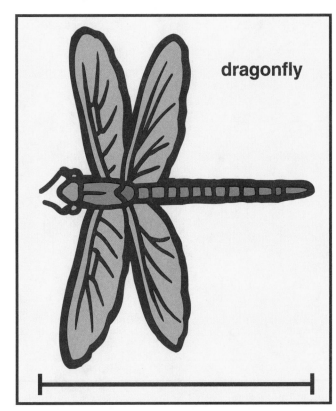

scorpion

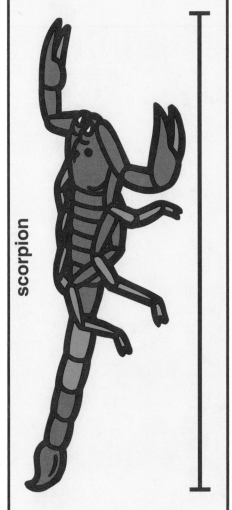

butterfly

spider

centipede

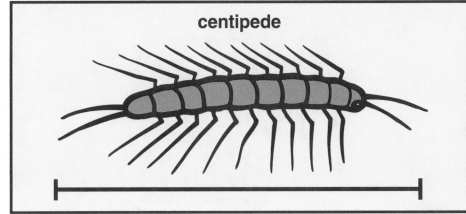

Creepy and Crawly Cards

caterpillar

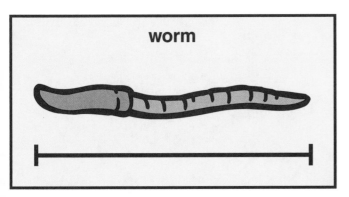

tick

bee

snail

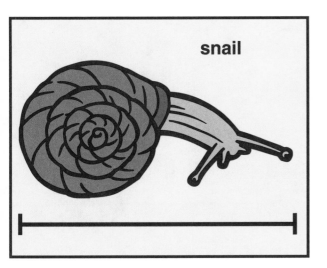

ant

silverfish

praying mantis

worm

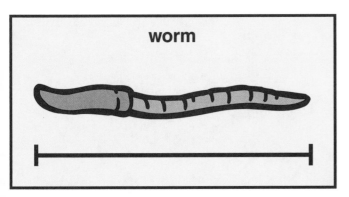

snake

#3170 Math Literacy Activities

Creepy and Crawly Answers

 ant = 1 inch (1") or about 3 cm

 bee = 2 inches (2") or 5 cm

 beetle = 3 inches (3") or about 8 cm

 butterfly = 2 inches (2") or 5 cm

 caterpillar = 2 inches (2") or 5 cm

 centipede = 4 inches (4") or about 10 cm

 cricket = 3 inches (3") or about 8 cm

 cockroach = 3 inches (3") or about 8 cm

 dragonfly = 3 inches (3") or about 8 cm

 earwig = 2 inches (2") or 5 cm

 flea = 1 inch (1") or about 3 cm

 fly = 1 inch (1") or about 3 cm

 grasshopper = 4 inches (4") or about 10 cm

 ladybug = 1 inch (1") or about 3 cm

 millipede = 4 inches (4") or about 10 cm

 mosquito = 2 inches (2") or 5 cm

 praying mantis = 3 inches (3") or about 8 cm

 scorpion = 5 inches (5") or 13 cm

 silverfish = 1 inch (1") or about 3 cm

 snail = 3 inches (3") or about 8 cm

 snake = 6 inches (6 ") or about 15 cm

 spider = 2 inches (2") or 5 cm

 tick = 1 inch (1") or about 3 cm

 worm = 3 inches (3") or about 8 cm

172

#3170 Math Literacy Activities

©Teacher Created Resources, Inc.

Rulers